Hamlyn
London · New York · Sydney · Toronto

LONDON

A portrait of Britain's historic capital

Fred Housego

endpapers Neon lights at Piccadilly Circus, a homing point for London visitors.

title spread The Houses of Parliament at night seen from across the Thames.

contents spread Trafalgar Square, so named after the Battle of Trafalgar in 1805. Nelson's column surmounted by the statue of Lord Nelson is at the front.

First published in 1982 by
The Hamlyn Publishing Group Limited
London · New York · Sydney · Toronto
Astronaut House, Feltham, Middlesex, England

Copyright © The Hamlyn Publishing Group Limited 1982

Reprinted 1983

ISBN 0 600 34294 8

Printed and bound by Graficromo s.a., Cordoba, Spain

Contents

Introduction

Maybe it's because I'm a Londoner

So goes the opening line of a very famous old song. Full of sentimental clichés it nevertheless gives a number of clues to what people feel about London. The main indication is in the word 'maybe', because you don't have to be a native of London to love her.

Dr Johnson, who came from Lichfield, was in his soul a Londoner. As everyone knows, he wrote the lines:

'When a man is tired of London
He is tired of Life.'

The capital has been a magnet for people from all over the world and it's their contribution that has made and shaped our city today. From the moment the Romans decided on the present site London has not stopped growing. First within the Roman boundaries then slowly but consistently along the highroads and lanes extending beyond to engulf hamlets and villages.

That growth is about people, people needing homes, people engaged in business and people making their way in the world.

From the earliest times people especially from Europe never ceased to be amazed by the colour, noise and richness of life in London. Such burghers as William Walworth who killed Wat Tyler and Dick Whittington excited the imagination with their undreamed of wealth.

Through the eyes of such people as Fitzstephen and John Stow the life of London from the Normans to Elizabeth I passes slowly by. Not only the monarchs and the magistrates but tradesmen, porters, inn keepers come

alive. It is also possible to trace the development of the city and in some cases mark the decline of the city's water and open spaces. Fitzstephen will mention a stream as having sweet sparkling water, by Stow's time in the sixteenth century it's referred to as a foul ditch, in one case, that of the river Fleet, the pollution was so offensive that by the eighteenth century it had to be culverted.

Today the river Thames and London itself are amongst the cleanest rivers and cities in the world. But a city's principal attractions are not usually the pollution free air or the cleanliness of its rivers important though such factors are in enhancing the quality of life.

For me the sheer pleasure of wandering around London comes from the way the capital is made up of dozens of small villages each with its own centre and character.

Soho with its cosmopolitan style Italian, Greek, French, Indian and Chinese interwoven and interspliced, living and working side by side. The feeling of sinister goings on amidst the clubs, restaurants and boutiques more apparent than real.

Chelsea is an upmarket village with a little of the Soho feel about it. King's Road is its main thoroughfare, a mixture of clothes shops and restaurants, but most people would agree that the biggest pastime in Chelsea is looking at and being looked at.

As the King's Road stretches west so the street goes through a gradual transformation from razzamatazz of the rag trade to antiques and upmarket fixtures and fittings for the average Georgian terraced house in the appropriate postal district.

Westminster, whilst officially a city, has that village feel. Admittedly instead of a village green or parish hall it has the Houses of Parliament, but a short distance from Parliament Square you can wander through quiet residential streets of period houses.

Here dress is more formalized yet people watching is still very popular, sometimes one can see a cabinet minister or a peer of the realm wandering along, perhaps to Number 10 Downing Street.

Just over a mile from the 'House' and you are in London's most exclusive neighbourhood – Belgravia. Lords and Ladies, cinema magnates, Texas and Saudi oil millionaires live in Regency splendour amongst embassies and consulates. Even the police station has flower baskets outside.

It is just these contrasts that make London for me. Pageantry yes, marching men, scarlet tunics and burnished armour, the state opening of Parliament, the Lord Mayor's show.

History by the bucket load, from Buckingham Palace to the Tower of London and St Paul's to Westminster Abbey. Theatre either classical or popular, concerts Beethoven or Bad Manners.

Art and culture, The National Gallery, the Tate, the Royal Acadamy, the British Museum, the list is infinite.

However even without all of the foregoing, highly attractive though they are, London would still be the only place for me. Parks and open spaces, a riot of colour in spring, green and seductive in summer, mellow and misty in autumn, bracing and brisk in winter, give London a sense of space and sanity. The street markets with their feeling of optimism and prosperity at a discount are contrary to the trend in the early 1960s making a come back. Places like Church Street now not only have the fruit and vegetable barrows but record stalls, shoe stalls and the ubitquitous antique and bric-a-brac stalls and minimarts. At Wembly the home of football, countless thousands of people spend Sunday morning amongst the stalls selling everything from shoes to model trains.

Leaving behind the crowded markets and following the canal towpaths it's soon easy to forget that London is all around you. From the elegant terraces surrounding Little Venice a short walk westwards and you can be up past Kensal Rise and into open spaces and the crowded silence of the area's countryside. Simply sitting on top of a London double-decker bus is a rare pleasure, especially when riding out through the suburbs spying on people's gardens and eyeing the mixture of parks and houses. And what of the pubs? Pubs with music, pubs with food, modern pubs, ancient pubs, a pub for every taste. Back to Dr Johnson again whose appalling eating and drinking habits were only exceeded by his love of London and his ability to distill the essence of the city's attractions into words, he said of taverns:

'No sir! there is nothing which has yet been contrived by man, by which so much happiness has been produced as by a good tavern.'

I couldn't agree more apart from our absurd licensing laws (I'd love to hear Dr Johnson voice his opinion on that matter) – the pubs taverns and inns, call them what you will, of London have proved impervious to change and are still a welcoming sight on a cold winter's night.

To list all the famous people who have lived in London and have enhanced life on earth as well as decorated the capital by their presence would take a book on its own. But the fact that they found in London a place in which they could work and live is a far more eloquent testimony to the infinite qualities of the 'Flower of cities all' as William Dunbar put it.

So returning to my opening sentence, you can be a Londoner by birth, by adopting or simply by just spending a few hours wandering around its streets. Being a Londoner is a state of mind not fixed by mortgage or rates, but by having an understanding of its eccentricities and oddities.

As Charles Dickens put it, himself a Londoner by spirit if not by birth –

'A roost for any bird'.

Central London

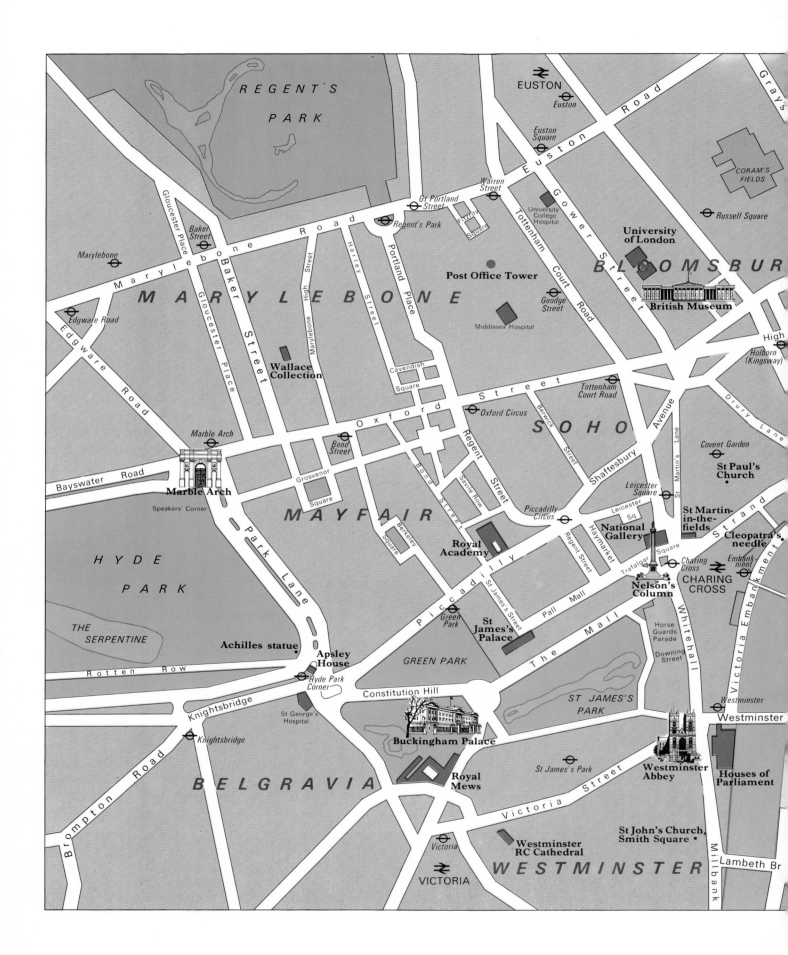

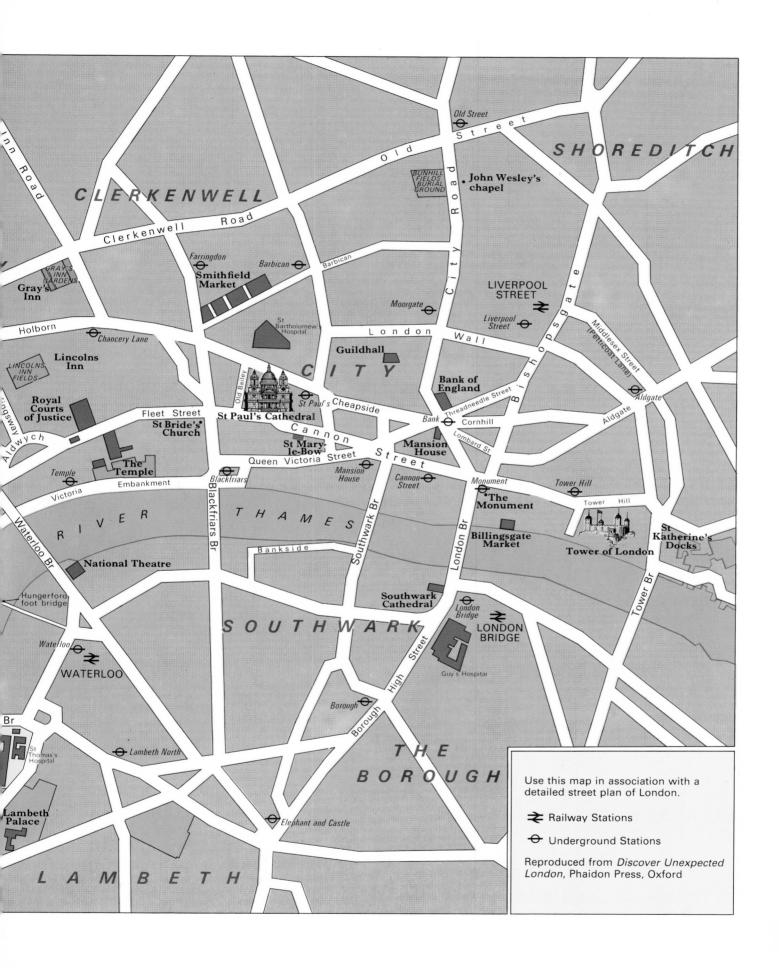

SHOREDITCH

Old Street

BUNHILL
FIELDS
BURIAL
GROUND
• John Wesley's chapel

CLERKENWELL

Clerkenwell Road

LIVERPOOL STREET

Farringdon   Barbican
Barbican

GRAY'S
INN
GARDENS
Gray's
Inn

Smithfield
Market

Moorgate   Liverpool Street

London   Wall

Holborn

Chancery Lane

St
Bartholomew's
Hospital

LINCOLNS
INN
FIELDS
Lincolns
Inn

Guildhall

CITY

Bishopsgate

Middlesex Street (Petticoat Lane)

Aldgate

Aldgate

Royal
Courts
of Justice

St Paul's Cathedral

Old Bailey   St Paul's   Cheapside

Bank of
England

Threadneedle Street

Bank   Cornhill
Lombard St.

Fleet   Street

St Bride's
Church

St Mary-
le-Bow

Cannon

Mansion
House

Aldwych

Temple   The
Temple

Queen Victoria Street   Street

Mansion
House

Cannon Street

Monument

Tower Hill

Tower   Hill

St Katherine's
Docks

Victoria   Embankment

Blackfriars

Blackfriars Br.

•The
Monument

Waterloo Br.

RIVER   THAMES

Bankside

Southwark Br.

London Br.

Billingsgate
Market

Tower of London

Tower Br.

National Theatre

Hungerford
foot bridge

SOUTHWARK

Southwark
Cathedral

London
Bridge

LONDON
BRIDGE

Waterloo

WATERLOO

High   Street

Guy's Hospital

Br

St
Thomas's
Hospital

Lambeth North

Borough

Borough

THE

BOROUGH

Lambeth
Palace

Elephant and Castle

Use this map in association with a
detailed street plan of London.

⇄ Railway Stations

⊖ Underground Stations

Reproduced from *Discover Unexpected
London*, Phaidon Press, Oxford

LAMBETH

The Tower of London

The beginnings of the Tower of London are shrouded in legend. Its position within the south east corner of the old Roman City walls led to the legend that Julius Caesar built it – Shakespeare used that in Richard III.

However, truth is stranger than fiction, not in the building of the Tower but in the events that were to take place within its expanding walls over the 900 years that followed from the construction of the White Tower (the oldest part of the fortress) in 1078.

Why was the tower built? Consider the situation in 1066. William the Conqueror had defeated Harold at Hastings, but the London contingent of the Anglo-Saxon Fyrd (or army) had retreated in good order to the sturdy walls of London. William approached London from Sussex via Canterbury and the south bank at Southwark. Instead of advancing direct across London Bridge he turned west, burning and destroying as he went to advertise his determination to put down any opposition.

Finally, crossing the Thames and moving towards London, William met the senior citizens of London at Berkhamstead. In return for recognition of London's privileges the Londoners accepted William as their king. But William needed to impress his new subjects and also he needed a strategic retreat in the event of rebellion. So the Tower was built to:

1. Overawe London.
2. Defend London's eastern approaches.
3. As a place from which to govern.

Over the centuries the Tower was expanded with curtain walls, ditches, a moat and a series of drawbridges and towers, to take its present shape. Technically it is a concentric castle. The Tower or, to give it's proper title, Her Majesty's Palace and Fortress of the Tower of London, is unique in that it can claim to be the oldest building in the world in continual use for the purpose for which it was built – arsenal, palace, prison, sometime zoo, royal mint, parish.

But it is its association with the famous and infamous that makes the Tower a must for visitors. Richard II abdicated his crown in the White Tower, Henry VI was murdered in the Wakefield Tower and the two princes were murdered in the Bloody Tower and buried at the foot of the staircase in the White Tower.

From the moment the Tudors ascended the throne the tower became even more sinister as a state prison. Sir Thomas More, Anne Boleyn, Catherine Howard, the poet Earl of Surrey, Lady Jane Grey, the Earl of Essex. The list is endless, each death a tragedy, occasionally a state necessity, never without a tinge of pathos. Many were judicial murders, none more so than that of Sir Walter Raleigh. An Elizabethan who had strayed into a different age he spent thirteen years in the Tower, becoming one of the sights of London. Even James I's son, the Prince Henry, criticized his father – 'only a king like my father could keep such a bird in a cage'. The list of the sufferers is infinite. The English historian and politician Macauley described the space in front of the parish church as 'the saddest spot on earth'.

Oddly enough the Tower was not as escape-proof as it has been made out to be. The first to escape was Ranulph Flambard, Bishop of Durham, who slid down a rope in 1100. Jesuits escaped, including a relative of Shakespeare's. Perhaps the most bizarre escape was that of Lord Nithsdale, a Scottish peer, who had chosen the wrong side in 1715. With the aid of his wife and a maid he escaped dressed as a woman. That wouldn't have been too remarkable except that Lord Nithsdale was over six foot tall and sported a bright red beard!

The Tower is a parish in its own right and today still carries on its age-old traditions. One such is Beating the Bounds. In every third year the choristers of St Peter Ad Vincula – the church within the Tower – and some of the children of people who live there go in procession around the parish boundaries and beat the thirty-one boundary markers. The ceremony is a reminder of the days when very few people could read and write and this was the only way of ensuring that future generations would know the limits of their parish. It was important because of certain privileges and obligations that parishioners had: tithe payments to the church, rights of grazing, fishing and use of common land. Originally it was the boys who were beaten at each boundary marker but today they beat the markers. Much more civilized!

Another tradition with a very long history is the Ceremony of the Keys. This takes place every evening at 10 pm when the Tower is being shut. Visitors may see the ceremony if they write first to the governor of the Tower. Five minutes before the hour, the Chief Yeoman Warder is escorted by a sargeant and three men whose job it is to help him close the three gates. When the keys return the escort is challenged by the sentry.

'Halt, who goes there?'
'The keys'
Whose keys?'
'Queen Elizabeth's keys'

The keys and escort then proceed through the arch under the Bloody Tower where they meet the entire guard. The guard present arms and the Chief Warder doffs his hat and shouts

'God preserve Queen Elizabeth'

The keys are then placed in the Queen's house for the night.

Visitors today find little signs of the violence, but ten minutes wandering around in the White Tower armoury gives a good many examples of the equipment needed to cause and survive assault. The Tower possesses one of the finest collections of arms and armour in the world. Henry VIII's armour is alone worth the visit – you can follow his progress from well-built young man to bloated and despotic monarch. Love him or hate him, you can't ignore him.

From grim reminders of its distant past to the inimitable, priceless and romantic vestiges of royalty, the Crown Jewels. Here too blood taints these sacred objects. The Koh-i-Noor diamond is said to bring death to any man who owns it; that is why it was given to Queen Victoria. In the Imperial State Crown is the Black Prince ruby, given by Pedro the Cruel to the Black Prince after the Battle of Najora in 1367. Yet, standing in front of such splendour, the only violence is the possible damage to your eyes.

Leaving the gloom of the safe vaults one's eyes are drawn to two living aspects of the Tower – Yeoman Warders or 'Beefeaters', who still wear Henry VII costumes and guide around the Tower with the assurance of Sir Lawrence Olivier on stage at the National Theatre. The other tenants of the Tower are the ravens, dressed a little more sombrely than their keepers but just as colourful in their fashion. Legend has it that should the ravens leave the Tower it would fall. No-one believes this legend but just to be on the safe side their wings are clipped.

It could be said that happiness is leaving the Tower. But satisfaction is having been there.

Opposite St John's Chapel in the White Tower – begun 1078. The finest example of early Norman church architecture in London. It's almost certain that every monarch from William II to Charles II would have worshipped here. It is associated with the Knights of the Bath from their foundation in 1399 by Henry IV.

Her Majesty's Fortress and
Palace of the Tower of London.
A concentric castle founded by
William the Conqueror on
Roman foundations it contains
examples of virtually every
architectural style from
Romanesque to Victorian
castling. The crown jewels, the
Beefeaters and the ravens are just
a few of its major attractions.

*The White Tower began in 1078
by Gundolf the Monk for
William the Conqueror. The
Tower has had its appearance
changed by the addition of
cupolas in Henry VIII's time
and the windows were remodelled
by Sir Christopher Wren.*

below *The Yeoman Warders of the Tower. Their uniforms are still as they were in Henry VII's time though it is thought that some wardens were guarding the Tower long before 1485.*

bottom *The Tower is a parish and to ensure that children would know their parish boundaries the ceremony of beating the bounds takes place on every third year. Boys from the chapel royal along with children who live in the* tower *visit thirty-one boundary markers. It used to be the custom to beat the boys now the boys merely beat the marker stones!*

opposite *The Tower Armoury. From Viking axes to the purely decorative armour of the Stuart period every age is represented. Illustrated is one of the many suits worn by Henry VIII in the Tower's possession.*

16

The City and St Paul's

I should begin by drawing a clear distinction between the City of London and London. The latter is that seemingly endless sprawl that is home to seven million people covering some 700 or more square miles, whilst the City of London – the area encompassed by the old city walls – is just over one square mile and has about 30,000 inhabitants.

Although not much remains of the old walls to distinguish London as we know it now from the City of London the distinction is maintained through the City's traditions. London is governed by the Greater London Council from County Hall sited by the Thames. The City is run by the Lord Mayor, Sherriffs, Aldermen and Common Councilmen of the city in the same way as it has been run for at least 800 years, a mixture of tradition and hard-headedness that has seen London change from a Saxon town huddled within old Roman walls through Empire to its present status as the financial capital of the world. It's a tradition that is jealously guarded.

Like so many great cities, London owes its existence to the Romans. They first tried to form a town at or near Westminster where the Thames was easily fordable but the area was too marshy. So, moving downstream, they found an area of shale overlaying the London clay – an ideal base for their stone buildings. There is ample evidence of the Roman presence at Leadenhall market, Cripplegate and Billingsgate where excavations on the Roman docks are taking place. The Romans stayed for nearly 400 years, making London one of the premier cities of the Roman empire. After their departure the city fell into decay until Alfred the Great (871–899) rebuilt the walls, but the days of imperial glory had past and London became a jumble of wattle and daub buildings straying over the grid pattern of the Roman town.

With the defeat of Harold at Hastings in 1066 and the accession to the throne of William I, England became more closely connected with France and Europe. Many of the old Saxon churches were rebuilt in stone and very soon London had over 100 churches and, more importantly, several monasteries – Benedictines, Carthusians and others. It was to be their organizations that were to lay the foundation of trade and the legal professions. By the fifteenth century London was a wealthy boisterous city, its burghers equal in power with the great magnates of the land. They financed the king's foreign wars and shared in government. There is a story that on returning from Agincourt to a great feast at the Guildhall, Henry V was greeted by Dick Whittington, Mayor of London. The King owed Whittington a large sum of money but to the king's relief Whittington publicly burnt the I.O.U!

Whittington was a member of the Mercer's Company and was expecting to increase and expand his business now that Henry had conquered France and reopened the trade links with Burgundy and the Low Countries. Still today you can get a feel of London's trade from the street names such as Cheapside (meaning market), Bread Street and Milk Street which need no explanation and Lombard Street where the bankers first set up shop.

Under the Tudors London assumed even greater importance as a trading centre, especially during the reign of Elizabeth I, and with Shakespeare, Marlowe, Fletcher and Beaumont over on the South Bank in Southwark, not only was London's importance increasing but there were writers to record it.

This explosion of trade was almost exclusively in the hands of the guilds and livery companies. They regulated trade set tariffs supervised quality-control of manufacture and most importantly controlled the government of the City.

Well into the seventeenth century London was still a medieval city, its buildings small, dark and insanitary, only here and there the great merchants' houses and the churches standing out. All that changed utterly when a fire broke out in Pudding Lane in September 1666. Known ever since as the Great Fire of London it burned for three days, destroyed two-thirds of the city, over fifty churches and marked the end of old London and the beginning of the urban sprawl that continues today. Spurred on, London burst its walls and moved out to join Wesminster, the Strand being the link between business and government.

It was during the eighteenth century with overseas conquest and ever-expanding trade that the institutions of the City that are so familiar today were founded. Today the income derived from their international trading earns a massive export surplus for the country known as invisible earnings because they are exporting a service rather than goods.

These city institutions such as the Bank of England, the Stock Exchange and Lloyds Insurance Brokers owe their prime position to their unrivalled expertise learned over the centuries. They have laid down the rules of trade finance and commerce that with only small variations have been the standard for such institutions throughout the world.

Standing on the highest point of land in the city is St Paul's Cathedral designed by Sir Christopher Wren. The present St Paul's was begun very soon after the Great Fire in 1666. The then old St Paul's was already in a state of disrepair and when the smoke cleared only the walls remained. The new church took thirty years to complete and those years were marked by continuous criticism of Wren by his enemies. However, he triumphed and St Paul's is a testimony to his skill, genius and patience.

Looking at the cathedral today it's difficult to believe that it is smaller than its predecessor. From the ground to the cross it is 365 feet but the spine of old St Paul's was 498 feet high.

On entering, the first impression is one of sheer size and of how un-English it looks with its glistening mosaic-covered ceilings and murals. Looking down the nave, the high altar under its baldachin is twentieth century and is a fine tribute to modern craftsmen. If one word sums up St Paul's it is craftsmanship. The skill of Grinling Gibbons whose subtle carvings in wood adorn the organ, the sheer beauty of Jean Tijou's iron gates, the mosaics of Sir William Richmond and of Salviati and Sir James Thornhill's monochrome paintings together with the dome form all make up a montage of artistry, skill and craftsmanship that is quite breathtaking. But even the majesty of a cathedral is there for people, people worshipping, people being baptized and people being married. The Prince of Wales and Lady Diana Spencer were married in the cathedral in July 1981, the first Prince of Wales to be married here since Prince Arthur son of Henry VII married Catherine of Aragon.

Within the crypt are the remains of such famous people as Lord Nelson, the Duke of Wellington and of course Sir Christopher Wren, and many memorials to politicians, military men, musicians and artists.

Today St Paul's has a world-famous choir school and one of life's great pleasures is to be in the cathedral during practice or full service: their voices do justice to their glorious surroundings.

opposite *Bank Junction, the very heart of the city. The Bank of England (left), the Royal Exchange (centre) and the Mansion House (behind right) jostle together representing money, trade and city government.*

previous pages *Looking west towards Tower Bridge. The river Thames, as someone said, is a 'ribbon of history'. Until the early part of the nineteenth century it was the City's highway.*

below *The west front of St Paul's Cathedral. The wedding of the Prince and Princess of Wales propelled St Paul's into the world's headlines, the great concourse awash with Tudor-like colour and ceremony.*

opposite *The nave, looking east to the high altar – mosaics murals and marble monuments cannot detract from Wren's masterpiece. An echo of Byzantium in London.*

following pages *The south face of St Paul's; 365 ft from floor to cross it still isn't as high as old St Paul's at 498 ft, the tower of which crashed in 1561.*

opposite *Looking at New Court it seems almost worthwhile becoming a barrister just to work in such historic surroundings.*

left *Wigs and gowns proclaim them as barristers. Frozen for a moment either coming from or going to argue on behalf of a client or prosecute a villain.*

Monastic Gothic by G. Street. The Royal Courts of Justice, handily placed just opposite The Temple. It is here that the newly elected Lord Mayor is presented.

The College of Arms was given its first charter by Richard III in 1484. The present building dates from 1671. It holds records of all coats of arms and pedigrees and its library is the finest of its kind in the world.

28

right *The boundary marker of the City of London, featuring a shield with the cross of St George and the sword of St Paul.*

right below *Apothecaries' Hall. Still licensing physicians today the present building dates from 1670; John Keats became a licentiate of the society in 1816. It is one of the most charming buildings in the City.*

below *Brick Lane in the heart of the East End naturally sells the local favourite dish, jellied eels and winkles. But it is mainly involved in the sale of new and secondhand electrical fittings.*

bottom *Leadenhall market, one-time site of Roman administration today it trades in game, poultry and other foods right in the centre of the City.*

below *Smithfield. The largest meat market in the world. Every day some 9000 tons of beef, pork, lamb and poultry as well as game food is on display for sale.*

bottom *A market since Anglo-Saxon times. Billingsgate supplies lobster and Dover sole as well as cod and haddock for fish and chips. This market is soon to move downstream but the buildings will be preserved.*

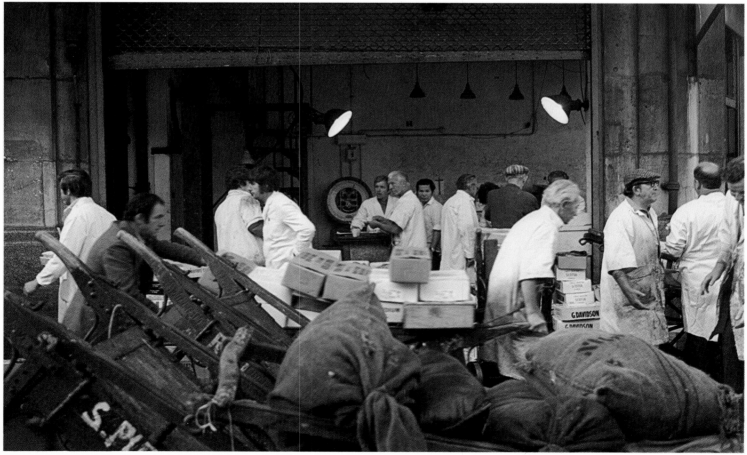

The City of Westminster

For over 900 years Westminster Abbey has been at the centre of British life and history. Edward the Confessor's great foundation is the final resting place of many of our kings and queens, princes and prelates, military and political leaders. Enter by the great west door and you are walking in the footsteps of every monarch crowned in the Abbey from William the Conqueror to our present queen. Indeed the Abbey has seen many a momentous occasion – coronations, royal weddings and royal funerals.

The present church was begun in 1245 to replace a Romanesque structure with a magnificent Gothic building to house the remains of Edward the Confessor. The architect, Henry of Reynes, died never realizing that it would be 500 years before the Western towers were added and his great design completed. The amazing feature of those 500 years of endeavour was that each succeeding architect kept faith with the original design even though styles had changed.

One of the many features of the Abbey are the various 'corners' dedicated to different aspects of British life. Socialists' Corner where Ramsey McDonald, the Webbs and others are commemorated. Scientists' Corner where Newton keeps company with Kelvin and Herschal. Musicians' Aisle where Purcell – 'a child of the abbey' – lies and Vaughan Williams and Orlando Gibbons are remembered. Statesmans' Aisle where the two parliamentary rivals, the stern-faced Gladstone and the smooth-tongued Disraeli, share a proximity in stone they never would have accepted in the flesh. Finally Poets' Corner a place where, as Washington Irving observed, visitors stayed the longest. And why not? Science progresses, politicians have, in the main, fleeting fame, but the English language as used by Chaucer, Spenser, Shakespeare, Keats, Shelley, Dickens and many others, remembered here has been granted immortality by their efforts.

But what of the Captain and the Kings? They too are very much in evidence. Henry III, the second great benefactor, lies close by the Confessor's shrine, near by is the classically beautiful tomb effigy of Eleanor of Castile by William Torel who, by his skilful hands, has rendered her ever young. Richard II and his wife, Anne of Bohemia, lie side by side. Richard was hardly a shining example of great kingship. Nevertheless he also was a great benefactor of the Abbey.

However, the king who must surely have the most spectacular tomb and chapel is Henry VII. The fan vaulted ceiling alone is worth walking miles to see. The graceful curves of the tracery give the stone a vein-like delicacy, complete with the heraldic banners of the Order of the Bath the whole chapel explodes with colour, fanning a perfect canopy for Henry's and his wife Elizabeth of York's tomb. Their effigies by Torrigiano are the finest renaissance sculptures in Britain. As an aside, it is interesting to note that when the tomb was opened in the 1860s the coffin of James I was found in there also! So much for the royal dignity!

In complete contrast to the famous and infamous Royals possibly the most impressive grave is the tomb of the Unknown Warrior whose burial here symbolizes the unspeakable suffering of the soldier in World War I.

'They buried him among the kings because he had done good toward God and toward his house.'

It is the only floor tomb that is never walked upon.

Leaving the Abbey via Poets' Corner one is immediately confronted by the Neo Gothic bulk of the Palace of Westminster otherwise known as the Houses of Parliament. Built on the site of Canute's palace which stood here in the eleventh century it is a site that has ever since been a centre of first royal government and now democratic government.

Its greatest treasure is Westminster Hall, laid out by William II in the eleventh century. It has the largest span of any wooden beamed roof in Europe, yet William when he saw it said 'they've merely built me a bedchamber'. The present hall owes its existence to Richard II and his great carpenter Hugh Herland and architect Henry Yevele who also worked on Westminster Abbey.

The Houses of Parliament are more than memorials to an illustrious past, though some might dispute that. They are the centre of British government which is carried out by the Houses of Commons and Lords. It is a bi-cameral system – upper and lower houses – the lower house is the Commons and consists of 635 elected members; the Lords consists of hereditary peers, life peers and bishops of the Anglican church. They are known as the Lords temporal and the Lords spiritual.

They sit in possibly the most impressive government buildings in the world. Designed by Sir Charles Barrie and August Pugin they reflect the sheer arrogant confidence of the Victorian age. From the benches of the house men like Disraeli, Gladstone and Palmerston spoke not only to Britain but to the world.

Though little of the world is coloured in empire pink today, the 'house' can often be the scene of near violent debates and visitors may sit in the strangers gallery either by queuing at St Stephen's entrance or by getting a ticket from their member of parliament.

Most MPs would agree that the buildings are too cramped for comfort but I doubt if any would want to sit anywhere else.

Taken as a whole the City of Westminster is an enigma. Taking its name from the Abbey, it contains the extremes of religion and politics, exclusive shopping and theatre to the glitter of the West End and the sex shops of Soho.

Whitehall, which links Trafalgar Square with Parliament, is given over almost entirely to government buildings. Tucked in a side street, almost as an afterthought, is No 10 Downing Street, home of the Prime Minister. Compared with the White House or the Elysée, a very modest address indeed, but in its time its doors have opened to admit some of the most famous names in world history. The first prime minister to live there was Sir Robert Walpole who was the first prime minister, he was followed by the Pitts, Lloyd George and Churchill and on up to the present day. Through war and peace right up until the 1950s this rather ordinary town house was the centre of an empire that was world wide.

Further up towards Trafalgar Square stands the Admiralty, just as Nelson would have known it before sailing to defeat the French at Trafalgar and to die at the moment of victory. Today it still controls Britain's navy on station throughout the world.

Nearly opposite Horse Guards Parade is the Banqueting House. Built by Inigo Jones between 1619–1622 it is in the Palladian style and is the first building of that style in England. Once inside, the ceiling demands immediate attention. By Rubens, the subject is the apotheosis of King James, the benefits of his government and the union of Scotland and England. Charles I for whom it was painted gave Rubens a knighthood and £3000 for his pains, and some twenty-seven years later on a wintry day in 1649 he walked through a window of that same building to his execution to become the 'Martyr King'.

opposite *Whilst MPs debate or merely nod off on the river terraces, a party of school children gets down to the serious business of a picnic lunch.*

Big Ben is the bell in the clock tower at the Houses of Parliament. During the war its out-of-tone notes signalled the BBC news throughout occupied Europe.

opposite above *The Chamber of the House of Lords – I've always been amazed that there can be Labour peers, yet here they sit facing their more orthodox Conservative counterparts. There are more than 1000 peers who are eligible to sit in the House.*

opposite right *Of all the Kings of England to have a statue outside Parliament Richard the Lionheart should be the least likely. Yet here he sits on his warhouse, a king who spent only six months of his ten years on the throne in this country.*

following pages *The Mother of Parliaments. The House of Commons and the House of Lords, two houses one elected the other hereditary.*

opposite *The Unknown Warrior. Laid to rest just inside the west door with the nave stretching out into the distance. A poignant reminder of man's mortality of the flesh and the immortality of his soul.*

left *Henry VIII Chapel. The flags of the Order of the Bath cannot overshadow the delicate beauty of the fan vaulted ceiling.*

The Collegiate Church of St Peter, Westminster. Setting for the coronation of our monarchs since 1066 and the place where many of them are buried.

Eleanor of Castile. Forever young and beautiful Eleanor's effigy shows her unravaged by old age. William Torel was the artist and he has created more than an image – a vision of loveliness.

following pages *The choir screen. Only the inner area of the gates dates from early times, the remainder was restored by Edward Blore in 1834. On the left is Isaac Newton, since his burial this area has been known as Scientists' Corner.*

46

opposite *Westminster
Cathedral. The premier Catholic
church in England. A mixture of
Byzantium and Romanesque just
along the road and a mere
ideological difference away from
Westminster Abbey.*

above *Inside the Cathedral. All
the splendour of Rome in
London. It's at its best during
the festival of flowers.*

above *It's been said that if you stand at Piccadilly Circus long enough you will meet everyone you've ever known, and also many others you don't know from Adam.*

right *Eros, London's first aluminium statue, a magnet for the young. At one time regarded as the hub of empire.*

opposite *Danny Kaye, Bob Hope, Maurice Chevalier are just a few of the great foreign stars who've graced the stage of the Palladium.*

previous pages *Buckingham Palace. The official London home of the Queen: not regarded as one of her more comfortable homes. It's said that during the early years of Queen Victoria's reign there was only one lavatory!*

above *Lambeth Palace. The official London home of the Archbishop of Canterbury. Begun by Hubert Walter, the first Archbishop to live there was Stephen Langton generally accepted as the author of Magna Carta.*

opposite above *The Banqueting House. Peter Paul Rubens' overwhelming ceiling dedicated to James I's memory by his son Charles I who walked to the scaffold from a window in this building in January 30 1649.*

right *St James's Palace. Built
on the site of a Leper hospital by
Henry VIII. It is from Friary
Court that the first proclamation
of a new sovereign is made.*

previous pages *Trafalgar Square is surrounded by interesting buildings such as the National Gallery and St Martin-in-the-Fields (right) possibly London's finest classical church designed by James Gibb.*

below *A curse or a pleasure? This lady obviously enjoys her encounter with the pigeons. But local office managers are less than happy about the bird droppings.*

bottom *St James's Park. An oasis of peace and a skyline to revive even the most jaded of visitors. Regarded by many as London's loveliest park.*

opposite *The finest site in Europe, Peel called it. Today Trafalgar Square is often the scene of demonstration. Every Christmas Norway presents a Christmas tree in gratitude for London's hospitality to their King and Queen in World War II.*

The West End

below *Trumpers of Curzon Street. The place for a very high class trim and shave – the 'by appointment' says it all.*

bottom *Bob Hope once said sometimes you can be lucky in London, the fog clears and you can see the rain. The fog is a thing of the past and the rain can be kept at bay with a fine traditional umbrella from Smith and Sons.*

Piccadilly Arcade. Cashmere, tartan, handmade shoes and silver purveyed with discretion don't you know!

Harrods. The top peoples' shop:
everything from tea bags to
tiaras. Every year they hold one
of the best sales in London.

Open Air London

Equipped with a decent pair of shoes, a map and an enquiring mind, London will reveal different facets to the normally accepted ones of history and ancient buildings.

Throughout Central London there are several parks – 'The lungs of London' – Hyde Park, Green Park and St James's. They are so close that they virtually overlap at Buckingham Palace. Bandstands, boating lakes, swimming – take your pick, either sit and listen, or sweat over a pair of oars or simply admire the statuary as you wander through the seasons. It is said that, to surprise children, the statue of Peter Pan was erected at night so they would discover it in the morning.

Possibly London's most beautiful park is St James's, bordering Horse Guards Parade, it has a bandstand, a beautiful lake and from the bridge a view of London's skyline that is stunning. Also the lake is home for a wide variety of wildfowl including pelicans. The park is an ideal place to watch the 'Bowler hats' of Whitehall taking a lunchtime stroll to feed the ducks.

To the north west of Central London is Regent's Park. Surrounded by the elegant Nash terraces, built for the Prince Regent at the beginning of the nineteenth century, the park is worth a day and an evening on its own. A fine boating lake – it featured in *The 39 Steps* with Kenneth More – is only part of the park's attractions. Within the inner circle is Queen Mary's Garden, a magnet for flower lovers, especially if you like roses. Close by is the open air theatre where, on fine summer evenings, Shakespeare's plays are performed. But Regent's Park's main claim to fame is the Zoological Gardens. The collection of mammals, insects, birds and amphibians is the finest in the world. The zoo really got off the ground when the Royal menagerie was shifted from the Tower of London in 1835 to join the Royal Zoological Society's collection. An ideal way to arrive at the zoo is by canal narrow boat from Little Venice, passing on the way Lord Snowdon's geometric aviary.

Whilst parks give a breathing space to a crowded city, it is the people who shape a city's character and give it that vital something that makes New York what it is and Paris also. Londoners can be seen at their best or their worst in the many street markets around both the inner and outer areas. Some are world famous, such as Petticoat Lane and Portobello Road. Fascinating and exuberant as these two markets are, because of their fame they are no longer truly representative as they once were.

No, to see a market operating as a market you have to go to places like Berwick Street in Soho. It is particularly good for fruit and vegetables but also has stalls selling books, clothes and a variety of other items. If you're feeling adventurous, then a short bus trip south of the river to Walworth and East Street market will give a genuine feel of a London fast disappearing.

Apart from such retail markets there are a number of wholesale specialist markets. The two that are most famous are Smithfield meat market, where some 9000 tons of meat is ready for sale at any time, and Billingsgate fish market, close by the Tower of London. Be prepared to get up early to see them in full flow. They are very closed communities where porters are usually second and third generations. In the case of Billingsgate visit it soon, because it is due to move down river.

From burly porters to London's crowded streets, the central thread is maintained by buskers or street entertainers. Plucking guitars, escaping from sacks, tap dancing or supervising performing budgerigars, the variety is infinite.

It's a tragedy that, unlike other foreign capitals, London until very recently frowned upon street entertainment as liable to cause an obstruction! Whether playing in the subways or performing to cinema queues they echo a time when street hawkers, fire eaters, jugglers and countless others earned their living on London's streets.

One place where buskers and street entertainers not only perform but are openly encouraged is Covent Garden. This was originally the wholesale fruit and vegetable market for London, but when the market moved to Battersea the buildings were carefully renovated and the many nooks and crannies leased out to shops, restaurants, wine bars and stalls selling everything from toys to meat and fresh bread.

There is also a transport museum and a bric-a-brac market. To me it seems rather twee but nevertheless the area is lively and appears to be popular with office workers and visitors. Perhaps being so new it needs time to get worn, comfortable and familiar. I feel that they have not yet exorcised the ghosts of the old market with its smells of fern, celery, plums, potatoes and all the other bits and pieces that go to make up an active wholesale market with a history that goes back over three hundred years. Shaw recognized this when he set some of Pygmalion in the market and made Eliza Doolittle a flower seller. When the play became 'My Fair Lady' some of the scenes were shot under the east portico of St Paul's church. Better known as the actors' church because of its many associations with the theatre – Ellen Terry's ashes are preserved there – St Paul's, designed by Inigo Jones, borders the west side of the market area giving a very classical look to the piazza-style layout of Covent Garden.

Returning to the parks, Hyde Park in particular is the stage for a uniquely British institution – Speakers' Corner – where Moslem shouts at Christian, communists debate with tories and the eccentric hold conversations with themselves free from censorship and control. If people-watching is as fascinating to you as serpentining through famous buildings, then its to places like Speakers' Corner that you will eventually find your way.

Street life is as vigorous, vulgar and pulsating in London as anywhere else in the world, merely by standing back and observing it or photographing it, you become part of it.

opposite *Formalized beauty, nature manicured, a quiet corner of Kensington Palace Gardens suitably correct for generations of nannies to perambulate with their charges.*

Band of the Life Guards at Hyde Park. The Edwardian era lives again as the band plays on. Have they relieved Mafeking yet?

bottom *The statue of Peter Pan in Kensington Gardens. J. M. Barrie lived a short distance away in Bayswater. Barrie is dead but the boy who never wanted to grow old has had his wish come true.*

Recline and decline into slumber in any of Central London's parks and let the world go by.

opposite *Berkeley Square. I doubt if any self-respecting nightingale would be caught dead singing here today simply because of the growl of the traffic, but the square at least on the west side boasts some fine eighteenth-century houses.*

below *A Midsummer Night's Dream comes true in Regent's Park open-air theatre.*

bottom *Penguin pool. It's not only the animals that are worth seeing at the London Zoo. Some of the architecture can be as interesting and as quirky as the inmates. 1930s.*

following pages *The Post Office Tower: man and nature combine to create a distinctive landscape. I think nature won.*

Pageantry and Traditions

The British love of pageantry is world famous and one of the many images of London will be of some best-remembered and colourful ceremony: Changing the Guard, Trooping the Colour, the State Opening of Parliament or any of the ceremonies of the City. Although they may first appear as spectacle laid on for tourists, these ceremonies infact represent a continuing link with the past so it is worth knowing something about the traditions behind these events in order to appreciate British pageantry to the full.

The State Opening of Parliament is the occasion when the sovereign officially opens the new session by summoning the House of Commons to hear the Queen's Speech from the House of Lords. To make known their independence the Commons first ignores the summons by slamming the door in the face of the Queen's messenger, Black Rod. Having made clear their independence they then proceed to the House of Lords to hear via the Queen's Speech what new legislation would be submitted to the Commons in the forthcoming session. Luckily, today this ceremony is televised to the nation, so millions can see in formalized fashion the independence of their members of Parliament from regal interference. This is a colourful reminder to the public of Parliament's long battle with Charles I and their long struggle to maintain their rights against subsequent monarchs.

Another occasion when royalty brightens up the summer scene in London is Trooping the Colour. This is a moment when all the Queen's horses and all the Queen's men parade before their sovereign on Horse Guards Parade on her official birthday.

To be precise the men on parade are the troops of the Household Cavalry, the Life Guards and the Blues and Royals and the men of the five guards' regiments – Grenadiers, Coldstreams, Scots, Welsh and Irish, they make up the Household division.

This ceremony of trooping the colour is a recollection of a time when battles were hand to hand affairs and communications between forces in battle could be confused and often lost entirely. To ensure that troops knew where to rally and regroup their regiments or even

earlier their particular Lord's colour would be displayed or 'trooped' along the line so that everyone could recognize it. Today it is a form of theatre that has lost its meaning as technology has taken over. Yet it is a reminder of the continuity of our society's institutions and besides all that it's a gorgeous and colourful treat for the eye.

Of course with a city that has been in existence since Roman times ceremony has become as much a part of it as the bricks and mortar that give the city its physical shape.

Every November a pageant takes place when the newly elected Lord Mayor proceeds in his golden coach from the Guildhall to the Royal Courts of Justice to be presented to the Lord Chancellor. This procession is called the 'Lord Mayor's Show' and the various floats and marches present a theme chosen by the new Lord Mayor. It can be industry, commerce, youth and so on, highlighting the benefits of the foregoing society. This parade also recalls the time over 700 years ago when the King having given the city the right to elect its own man demanded that he present himself for the King's approval. In earlier times the procession went to Westminster by water.

Such events are justly world famous and draw vast crowds from home and abroad and because of this they are carefully organized and widely publicized. However, throughout the year in London many traditions continue virtually unknown to most people. One such occasion is the Lord Mayor's visit to St Andrew Undershaft to replace a quill pen in the alabaster hand of John Stow on the anniversary of his death. John Stow was one of London's greatest historians, it was said of him that he 'shackled the fabric of London's history' together, and rightly he is honoured annually by London's first citizen.

Another colourful occasion that is a remembrance of events that took place over 400 years ago is Oak Apple Day at the Royal Hospital Chelsea. This is held on 29 May to celebrate the founder's – Charles II – birthday. The oak apple sprig recalls Charles hiding in an oak tree near Boscbel after being defeated at the battle of Worcester in 1651. To en-

sure a feeling of warmth for their founder the Chelsea pensioners receive double rations, a very practical tradition.

Returning to the city, once a year at the Royal Courts of Justice on 23 October the city corporation pays rent on two long-lost properties: one the 'moors' in Shropshire and the other the 'forge' at St Clement Danes. For the 'moors' the rent is two faggots cut with a bill-hook and a hatchet and for the other property the rent is six horseshoes and sixty-one nails, these rents are collected by the Queen's Remembrancer. You can go along to the law courts to see this ceremony as visitors are admitted.

London being on a river there are a number of traditions associated with the Thames. In 1715 Thomas Doggett was so delighted with the Hanovarian Succession that he gave money to fund a race for watermen, this has become known as Doggett's Coat and Badge. The race is from London Bridge to Chelsea against the tide, a distance of four and a half miles. The winner has the right to wear the coat of scarlet and the large silver badge on the right arm depicting a rearing horse, the emblem of the Hanovarian.

And so it goes on, Lord Mayors parade in medieval splendour, judges clutching nosegays open the law terms at law courts, sympathizers place a wreath at the foot of Charles I statue in Trafalgar Square and Horse Guards face the cameras in Whitehall.

Virtually all of London's old established institutions have traditions and ceremonies of some kind and many are accessible to the general public.

Perhaps today grown men and women in some form of fancy dress do appear to be a trifle eccentric if not archaic, yet as aircraft go faster, as satellites beam the four corners of the world into our living rooms it's a comforting thought that officialdom can and does set aside the time to maintain and uphold our ancient traditions. They may be pointless exercises in colour and yet they are continuing threads showing us where we came from.

Opposite Some of All the Queen's Men, changing the guard. With Buckingham Palace as the dackdrop the guards' band huff and puff through their repertoire.

A tranquil moment at Chelsea hospital.

The ultimate 'Done our bit' club. Chelsea pensioners on Oak Apple Day.

opposite *Horse Guards Parade. Mounted, burnished and polished a daily cavalcade that draws visitors in their thousands.*

opposite *London's first citizen the Lord Mayor in his fairytale coach arrives outside the Law Courts.*

below *Opening of Law term: Lord Chief Justice. A full-bottomed wig and formal robes do not detract from the clear purpose of dispensing justice.*

bottom *The Honourable Artillery Company form up for the Lord Mayor's Show. They are the oldest military formation in Britain and owe their existence to Henry VIII.*

below *The Lord Mayor's Sword bearer in full ceremonial dress.*

Royal Ceremonial

right *Trooping the colour. The Queen's official birthday and a moment of unrivalled colour and majesty.*

below *Held in the grounds of the Royal Hospital the Chelsea Flower Show is regarded as the highlight of both the professional and amateur gardeners' year.*

opposite top *Symbols of sovereignty. Imperial State crown, ampulla and spoon, sceptres, annulets and jewelled sword.*

opposite bottom *The official opening of Parliament by the Sovereign. The Queen makes a speech to both houses of parliament written for her by the government outlining proposals for the new parliamentary session.*

Museums and Monuments

Given the history of our imperial past it was inevitable that wherever and whenever Britain extended her sway, she also collected vast amounts of plunder, gifts and artefacts. Over the years these remnants of conquest, added to by treasures from our own land, oscillated towards national collections. From the middle of the eighteenth century onwards the British invented the 'Grand Tour' a way for young men of means to broaden their education. When they returned they inevitably brought with them works of art, furniture, procelain, carpets and so on. Many of our Country Houses owe their contents to such acquisitions.

Of all the museums in London, the British is *the* museum. The present building dates from 1823-25 and is justifiably regarded as one of the world's great collections. The museum began in 1753 and was based on the Cottonian Collection presented to the nation in 1702 by Sir Robert Cotton. Since that date it has grown and grown through bequests, purchases and discoveries. It would be fair to say that the British Museum is the study of a lifetime but to mention just some of the exhibits will give an indication of its riches and the variety of mankind's activities from prehistoric to modern times.

The Rosetta stone for example, which paved the way for the deciphering of Egyptian hieroglyphics by a Frenchman, Champollion. The Sutton Hoo treasure, a magnificent collection of gold and niello work from a seventh-century grave. The museum is particularly rich in Roman remains, collections such as the Mildenhall treasure, fine examples of Roman silver – good enough to be used again today. Possibly the greatest treasure is the Elgin Marbles. They once adorned the Parthenon, but now they are a silent citizen of London. The Reading Room of the British Library at one time was home to Lenin, Marx and many others who would one day change the world. It still receives a copy of every book, pamphlet and periodical printed in Britain. This area has access restricted to students and those doing research.

However, on general display are such rarities as Nelson's battle plan at Trafalgar, Scott's diary written very shortly before he perished at the South Pole and Shakespeare's signature. Also the Lindisfarne Gospels and the Codex Siniaticus, presumed to be the second oldest bible in the world. The list is nearly endless – poems from the dark ages, early printed material and illuminated manuscripts fill case after case.

Apart from such a blockbuster as the British Museum there are smaller collections such as the Wallace Collection in Manchester Square. What is unusual about this museum is that it is the reflection of one family's taste, that of the marquesses of Hertford. The treasures are displayed in Hertford House, the former London home of the family, and the collection is static, that is nothing can be added or taken away. A visit here reveals a bewildering array of art works of world renown such as *The Laughing Cavalier* by Frans Hals, Rembrandt's portrait of his son Titus, works by Rubens, Watteau and Velasquez. Added to this is an excellent collection of European armour, porcelain, sculpture and bronze work.

If such a catalogue of possessions is too much to absorb or simply if history bores you, then London has a museum for every fancy, from pianos to dolls and steam engines to dinosaurs. They are housed in local collections such as the Geffrye Museum in East London to the Natural History section of the British Museum in a building that dwarfs the Cromwell Road. There are small collections dedicated to one man or one discipline – one is the Dickens Museum in Doughty Street, the house where Charles Dickens lived and wrote some of his books such as *Pickwick Papers*.

Virtually every borough has its history collection or art gallery – one such is Dulwich where a fine selection of Flemish paintings can be seen.

When the varied charms of the great collections pall, then there are always those other great Imperial reminders to be visited – our monuments. In 1851 the Great Exhibition was held in the Crystal Palace, then in Hyde Park. Coinciding with the opening up of the suburbs by railway the exhibition was a resounding success. The resulting profits were such that they were able to build the Royal Albert Hall, recalling in its name the Prince Consort and husband to Queen Victoria, who had been the driving force behind the event. Opposite is the Albert memorial, magnificent Victorian Gothic – a remembrance of the exhibition, with Albert reading a copy of the catalogue of items on display in the Crystal Palace. It's revealing that of all the world's fairs and other similar events held since that event in 1851, it was the only one to make a profit – all the others lost money!

Look anywhere else in London and if there's an open space you can bet that there'll be a statue. Trafalgar Square or Parliament Square, Kings, statesmen, warriors and famous foreign leaders can be found. Some quite magnificent, like Charles I at the top of Whitehall, or the strange statue of General Smuts who, someone said, looks like he's ice-skating towards Westminster Abbey.

One of the most poignant memorials in London is the Cenotaph (meaning empty tomb). Originally it was made of plaster for a victory march in 1919 but the public response was such that it was replaced by the present stone structure designed by Sir Edwin Lutyens for the Armistice service on 11 November 1920.

Finally, if ever concrete evidence was required of English eccentricity then one need look no further than Marble Arch, which was designed as the entrance to Buckingham Palace but popular mythology has it that it was too narrow for the state coach, so now it stands in splendid isolation at the north east corner of Hyde Park – an entrance to nowhere!

opposite Prince Albert the Prince Consort sits for all eternity perusing the catalogue of the Great Exhibition of 1851. It was his idea to bring together the best industrial products and art of the nineteenth century from all over the world to stimulate British industry.

previous pages *The Royal
Albert Hall. Home of the Henry
Wood Concerts better known as
the 'Proms'. Also scene of many
sporting events especially boxing.*

above *Admiralty Arch yet
another memorial to Queen
Victoria, now the entrance from
Trafalgar Square to the Mall.*

opposite top *Boudicca or
Boadicea, Queen of the Iceni, her
horse rears up almost as if it can
smell the water of the Thames
passing under Westminister
Bridge.*

right *The Queen Victoria Memorial known to generations of cab drivers as the 'Wedding Cake' because of its sugar icing look.*

The Cenotaph. It means empty tomb and
stands as a permanent reminder of the carnage
of World War I. On the nearest Sunday to
11 November the Queen, the Prime Minister
and representatives of the armed services place
wreaths of poppies here.

Dickens House. Doughty Street is only one of
many houses lived in by Dickens, but this is
the only one left. It is now a museum
dedicated to him.

Sir Walter Raleigh. He stands in Whitehall near where he was executed and close to the Admiralty.

opposite *The Imperial War Museum, Lambeth. Considering that its exhibits are all the result of wars, it is perhaps fitting that the building was at one time the lunatic asylum Bedlam.*

left *The Monument. Built in remembrance of the Great Fire of London by Sir Christopher Wren. It stands a few yards from where the fire started.*

below *The Museum of London stands within the Barbican a massive complex of housing, pubs, theatres and garden. The museum contains a wide variety of historic items associated with London.*

Churches

In an age when church attendances have fallen so dramatically that many have closed and parishes have amalgamated, it is difficult to imagine the London of the sixteenth century with the spires, towers and crosses of over 100 churches breaking the skyline, serving a population numbered in thousands, not the millions of today.

Like so many churches throughout the christian world, the foundations of these London churches are hedged round with legends, dimly discernable saints and visions. As Rome changed its pagan gods for christianity so that change permeated to the fringes of empire. England had already had two christian martyrs in Alban and Amphibilius, but with Constantine martyrdom became a thing of the past, at least as far as official Roman policy was concerned. In the British Museum there are a number of indications of the modification of pagan temples to christian worship. Its possible that some of the city churches are late Roman foundations.

However, the first major and systematic incursion by missionaries into London came with St Augustine, or rather his emissary Mellitus in 606. While that first approach was cooly received by the Saxons – more because of Mellitus and his patrician ways than the crudeness of the locals – it began an unbroken connection right up until the reformation. A thousand years in which churches and monastic foundations proliferated. In 607 St Paul's Cathedral – old St Paul's – was begun. By the thirteenth century most of London's churches were in existence, their styles a mixture of Romanesque and early English architecture. However, with the great fire of London nearly all of them were destroyed including St Paul's. It is to that catastrophe that we owe the skyline familiar to Londoners right up until the 1950s and the advent of the tower block.

In the rush to rebuild London one name is pre-eminent – Sir Christopher Wren. Church after church bears his imprint, an elegant spire here and a reducing tower there, each one different and yet possessing a 'Wren' look. Along with Wren you continually encounter Grinling Gibbons, the great wood carver whose limewood swags grace many an organ loft. It would seem that Wren was lucky on two counts: firstly he was given

the right circumstances, near total destruction, secondly he was surrounded by gifted craftsmen. Francis Bird, who sculpted the pediment over the west front of St Paul's, Nicholas Stone the great stone mason and many others. Their work survived until the next great fire, that of the blitz in 1940. Today many of those churches that stood for 300 years and fell in a heap of rubble in seconds have been lovingly and carefully restored. I'm sure even the meticulous Sir Christopher would approve.

Even through two major conflagrations some early churches survived, in the first instance because of their position in the city and secondly sheer luck. Most of the churches that came unscathed through 1666 were in the north east corner of the city or outside its walls. One such is St Bartholomew the Great, all that remains of a great priory founded in 1123 in the reign of Henry I. It still has the uncomplicated solidity of its Norman style almost unsullied by later hands. It's a younger brother of St John's Chapel in the Tower. St Bartholomew's started as a result of a vision had by Rahere, possibly a court official. It is said that after the death of Henry I's son William, Rahere went on a pilgrimage to Rome, whilst there he caught malaria and during his illness he had a vision of St Bartholomew who told him that when he returned home he should build a hospital. On his return he recounted his tale to Henry and was given land at Smithfield just outside the city walls. Later the priory hospital was granted a charter to hold a fair, the famous Bartholomew fair which still exists in part today as Smithfield meat market. With the dissolution of the monasteries the priory lost its great lands and influence. It fell into disrepair and for a time it was home to a blacksmith's a non-conformist chapel and printers where Benjamin Franklin worked. It is to me a perfect example of the grandeur of history, mixed with the simple needs of a parish church both entwined with today's community. It is still the guild church of the butchers' company.

Each London church is an integral part of the patchwork quilt of London's history. St Olave's, for example, was well known and often visited by Samuel Pepys, who is buried in the churchyard. Pepys like Wren is a name woven into the tapestry of London's history. St Olave's was his favourite church but he

often travelled to other churches to listen to sermons and eye the maids and ladies in the congregation – Pepys was a renowned womanizer. He watched the Great Fire from the church of All Hallows by the Tower and was a leading figure in pressing the government to take action to limit the spread of the flames.

Incidentally, it was at All Hallows that John Quincy Adams the sixth President of the United States of America was married whilst he was the ambassador to the court of St James. Also William Penn the founder of Pennsylvania was baptized in the church.

Another city church with an American connection is the Holy Sepulchre by Holborn viaduct, where Captain John Smith who was rescued by Pocahontas and was Governor and Admiral of Virginia lies buried. There was also a tradition which lasted well into the eighteenth century of giving convicted felons on their way to Tyburn for execution a posy of nosegays, perhaps a case of a man carrying his own wreath!

Parts of the Holy Sepulchre date from the fifteenth century, but most of it was rebuilt, like so many other churches by Wren in 1670–77.

At the same time as he was rebuilding here in Holborn he had begun work on what is, apart from St Paul's, his masterpiece, St Stephen, Walbrook. Its dome is sixty-three feet to its summit and forty-five feet in diameter at its widest part. It was probably an experiment for the much larger dome of St Paul's, but considering how small the church, is Wren has given the interior an amazing sense of space.

Whether magnificently rebuilt by Wren or radically renovated and restored after war damage London's churches are central to the fabric of the city's history. Each church tells a story, each has some treasure in stone or wood carving or tomb effigy dedicated to some city worthy. You can traverse the city in a day but to know London's churches is a lifetime's pursuit and a lifetime's pleasure.

opposite *Interior of St Bride's. The journalist's church, situated close by Fleet Street it was also where Samuel Pepys was baptized.*

St Pancras Church. Built in the 1820s the pillars are in the shape of caryatyds after the Greek fashion.

opposite *St Ethelburga's, Bishopsgate. The church is almost certainly an Anglo-Saxon foundation.*

below *John Stow's bust in St Andrew Undershaft. Each year the Lord Mayor replaces the quill in his hand with a new one. A fitting tribute to one of London's greatest historians.*

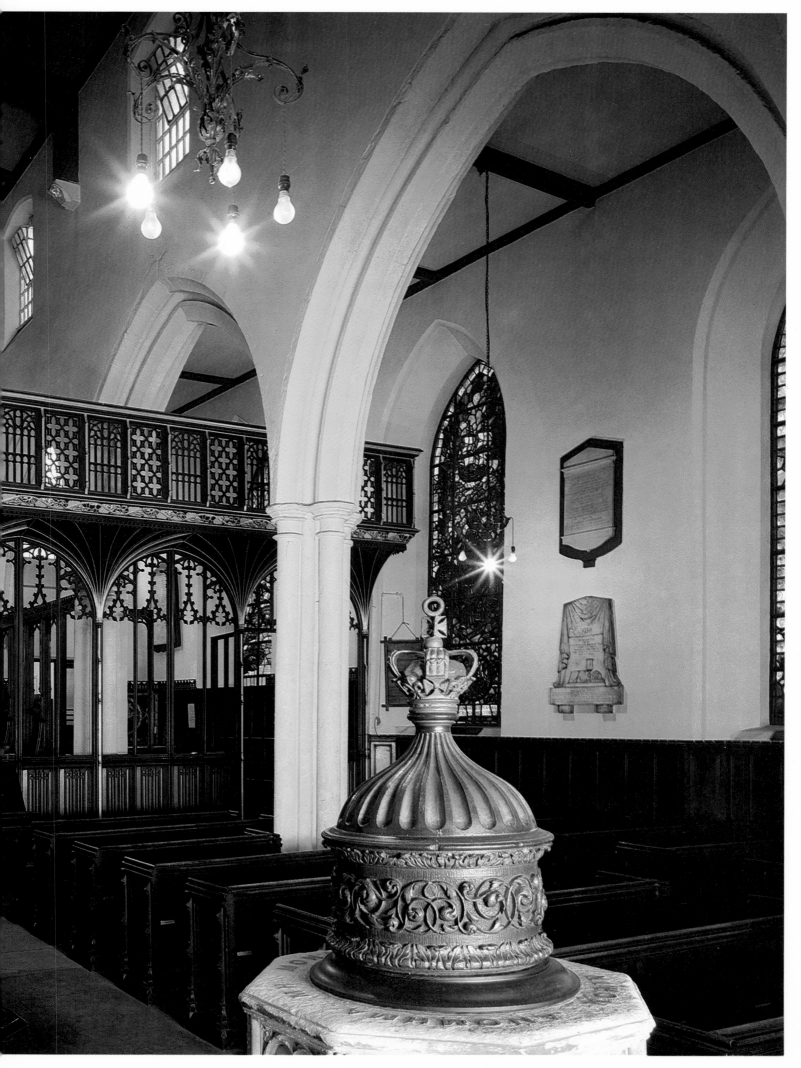

previous pages *The Brompton Oratory. Founded by Cardinal John Henry Newman, writer of the* Dream of Gerontius. *The building is in the Italian baroque style.*

right *Font carved in marble by Grinling Gibbon. St James's Church, Piccadilly – one of the few Wren churches built outside the City. Restored after war damage, the spire is of reinforced plastic.*

Roof boss at Southwark Cathedral – the Devil swallowing Judas Iscariot. A cathedral that casts its shadow over Borough Market and Bankside. Nearby was the site of the Globe Theatre and Shapespeare's brother is buried here.

opposite *Rahere's tomb in St Bartholomew the Great. In silent repose, he lies in medieval splendour.*

The River Thames

In any list of longest, widest, deepest or fastest, the River Thames would come nowhere. Yet, along with the Nile, it is possibly the most famous waterway in the world. Why? It didn't take years to discover the source; it wasn't the cradle of civilization; yet, as it rolls slowly down from the Cotswolds into the tidal basin, it somehow exhibits many of England's traits and characteristics. From honey-stoned hamlets through 'posh' riverside towns and into the Pool of London where abandoned wharves, moored ironclads of an imperial past and historic monuments form a montage of comments on centuries of London's central position in world history.

Today the river is a mere shadow of its former self. Where once the 'pool' had all the swagger and arrogance of a music hall comic calling himself the 'Breadbasket of Britain' it is now a genteel old man recollecting its robust youth in a collection of disused docks and casually abandoned barges. But for the first-time visitor it is still a magnet for those in search of something British. Returning to the Nile, just as the pyramids are etched on everyone's mind, I wonder how many miles of celluloid have frozen the image of tower bridge, either with bascules raised or lowered?

Leisure has taken over from industry and trade, partly because of the changing nature of shipping, partly because of the river shape. Upstream is the Oxford and Cambridge boat race. Further down, less academic, yet no less worthy, men battle for Doggett's coat and badge since the beginning of the eighteenth century. Alongside, hotels and offices shoulder aside the nineteenth-century palaces of commerce. But in St Katherine's Dock the very best of yester-year has been adapted for today's needs. Telford's elegant warehouses have been converted into an exhibition centre, with shops, flats and a marina. It has also become a floating maritime museum with HMS Discovery, the Nore lightship, and many other craft that were once as common on the river as sparrows on our streets. Its close proximity to the Tower of London makes it a perfect extension to this historic riverside area.

Further down all is quiet. The main dock area is dead, only the occasional riverside pub – Prospect of Whitby, Town of Ramsgate – gives some small indication of yesterday's flavour.

On a sombre note, it was at Wapping Steps that convicted pirates were chained until three tides had flowed over their bodies. Now only the beer flows and the river is no longer the distributor of rough justice.

Apart from piracy, crime on the river was endemic with even ships' captains and customs men being involved. Such exotic sounding villains as 'heavy horse-men', 'light horsemen' and 'mudlarks' carried out their pilferage on such a scale that the various dock owners formed their own police force, the fore-runner of the river police. Now there are no ships to steal from and the river police in their fast launches are sometimes the only boats moving on a vast empty river.

From Chelsea to the East End the river is an ever-changing scene. The ideal way to see the riverfront is from the river, but don't be deterred from walking. From Chelsea Reach to the City much of the waterfront is accessible to the casual stroller.

For example, the finest point to see the Houses of Parliament from is on the south bank close by Lambeth Palace. Further down you can stroll along by the river in front of the Royal Festival Hall and the National Theatre. The Victoria Embankment with its broad highway takes you by various government buildings and Cleopatra's Needle. Towards the East End the walks may be less majestic but with garden areas wedged between crumbling warehouses, the river here too has a certain charm.

As well as the main river London is built over many rivers such as the Fleet, Westbourne, Wandle and the Walbrook. The only time these rivers become visible is when they flow into the Thames. Today they are almost forgotten and yet they were very important in their day and helped to shape the city.

One area of London's waterways that can still be seen and enjoyed are the canals.

From the middle of the eighteenth century until well into the nineteenth century the canals were the industrial highways. Until the opening of the railways the narrow boats and the boat people formed a separate community. They brought merchandise and raw materials down from the midlands into the Port of London via the Grand Union and Grand Junction canals.

Today those narrow boats are eagerly sought after as holiday homes and many of the areas through which the canals pass are very fashionable, such as Little Venice. A long way from the days when it was known to my mother as 'Rat Island'!

Each bridge is an ideal vantage point to see London's skyline, especially Waterloo: County Hall, Royal Festival Hall, National Theatre and in the distance St Paul's. If London is the Queen of cities then Wren's dome is surely her crown. Many of the bridges have featured in the writings of people such as Wordsworth – 'a view from Westminster Bridge' – and as far back as the Viking age some-one wrote

London Bridge is falling down

Gold is won and Bright Renown London Bridge was the first bridge over the Thames and for centuries it was one of the sights of Europe with its houses all along its length. On the bridge were displayed the heads of people convicted of treason.

That bridge and its successor are no more. The last one is now in Lake Honasu in the USA.

Amongst the many artists who chose to paint views of the river the most famous was Canaletto. Whilst he may have given the weather a very Italian feel he did convey the majesty of the river and its effect on London. His works are as much historical records as they are works of art, showing the skyline, so different from today.

Another surprise that awaits the first-time visitor, or for that matter even native Londoners, is how twisting and winding is the river. Stand on Lambeth Bridge and look along the water course and you will be looking north or south, not east or west.

Through camera lens or open eyes there are certain sights that must not be missed. HMS Belfast, a veteran of World War II rides in gentle retirement opposite the Tower of London. Her heavy guns, if ever they transcribed an offensive arc around the 'Pool' would lob nine-inch shells as far away as Hampstead. She shared in the destruction of the Scharnhorst and acted as command vessel at the D' Day landings. Now, like the Tower, she is out of place in the age of the micro chip, yet like the Tower there is an aura of strength that can only be felt by a walk on the deck.

opposite H.M.S. Belfast permanently moored close by Tower Bridge. Whenever a warship pays a visit to London it ties up alongside her.

St Katherine's Dock. Here is a wide collection of retired craft of all shapes and sizes from Thames barges to H.M.S. Discovery used by Scott.

Once a bustling dock full of ships unloading the produce of the world, now it is a mooring for yachts and cruisers owned by people who would never have ventured here fifty years ago.

bottom *A Thames sailing barge passes gently by distant St Paul's, a reminder of a long gone age.*

The National Theatre.
Considering London's position in
the world of drama it's amazing
that it is only in the last few
years that Britain has attained a
National Theatre. It has three
theatres on one of the finest sites
in London.

*Looking like an upturned table
the power station is a timely
reminder of the river's more
workmanlike face.*

Art Exhibition on Board Now

opposite *Floating Museum by the South Bank.*

left *Winner of the Doggett's Coat and Badge Race. The race has been run ever since 1716 in honour of the Hanovarian succession.*

below *The River Thames is only one aspect of London's waterways. These narrow boats on Regent's Canal recall the heyday of Britain's canal system.*

following pages *A rare sight today but it has been estimated that the bascules have been raised over 100,000 times since the bridge was built.*

The Head of the River race which takes place a week before the Oxford and Cambridge race.

bottom *The Embankment. On a warm day an ideal place to pursue one of life's great pleasures, watching the river flow.*

All aboard the Skylark! From Westminster to Greenwich the ideal way to see the river.

Outer London

If, after the claustrophobia of inner London, even the parks of the town afford insufficient air then the suburbs with their heathlands, open spaces and historic houses will give your lungs plenty of exercise and another aspect of London life which is completely divorced from the dizzying rush of the centre.

Hampstead Heath, six or seven stations on the underground, is a mixture of heathland, gentle woodland, meadows, ponds and parks. Keats lived there, Constable painted there, so did Romney. It has been the retreat of artists, musicians, poets, writers and theatrical people ever since. On Bank holidays artistic Hampstead goes underground and it becomes 'appy 'ampstead as the fair takes over and the greenery shudders to the sound of pop music, big wheels and the shocking pink of candy floss.

As if to add a further contradiction to the already confused picture, a short walk towards Highgate reveals Kenwood House in all its pastoral glory, overlooking a lake and a false bridge it is my ideal of an English country house, it almost floats in the early morning mists. How fortunate to have woken up on clear summer mornings in this house 200 years ago! Within, all is classical Adam design with a library of stunning beauty. Added to the Flemish and other paintings the house, now in the care of the GLC, is one of the great treasures of England.

At Chiswick house in west London, Lord Burlington created a meeting place rather than a residence in the style of the Rotunda by Palladio at Vincenza. The restoration spanning ten years is a work of genius with delicate cornices and gilt decoration of infinite delicacy creating spell-binding images of the wealth of aristocracy. As if Chiswick wasn't enough, within a few miles at Brentford is Syon House. Originally the property belonged to the Duke of Somerset, protector of Edward VI, after his execution it passed to his successor in power, the Earl of Northumberland. In 1750 the then Duke of Northumberland commissioned Robert Adam to refurbish and remodel the house. Given carte blanche, Adam not only tackled the building but

designed the furniture and carpets as well as all the decorations. The Long Gallery in particular is Adam at his best. Furniture, floor coverings and finely decorated ceilings all in perfect harmony.

Of course, today as London spreads ever outwards these grand palaces of the high-born have lost their rural seclusion, but a hint of life in west London during that era can still be seen in the charming eighteenth- and nineteenth-century houses and cottages by Kew Bridge at Strand-on-the-Green. Admittedly it is a humbler way of life than stately-home society but in its balconied river-fronted homes, Strand is as much a part of the great Georgian age as any classical or baroque mansion.

This quadrant of London's suburbs is particularly rich in reminders of royal patronage and aristocratic aspiration. Describing an arc from Chiswick through Brentford on south west to Richmond and Petersham, you find a variety of richly decorated houses and spacious parks. In part they owe their existence to the river which bisects our imaginary arc and also to the Great West Road leading out to Windsor and on to Wales.

Richmond, close to the river, was given its name by Henry VII, called after his Dukedom at Richmond in Yorkshire. Today the park, which used to be a royal hunting park, still has reminders of the chase in the deer that wander freely, its meadows and open spaces and there's plenty to wander – some 2300 or more acres. Within this vast acreage stands White Lodge dating from the 1720s. It is associated more with royalty of recent times – Queen Victoria stayed here for a while, so did Edward VII, his grandson the Duke of Windsor was born here. Today it forms part of the Royal Ballet school but parts are open to the public at advertised times.

Nearby is Ham House, its austere exterior concealing within some of the richest decoration of any houses in Britain. Many of the furnishings date from the time of the Duke of Lauderdale, a close adviser to Charles II.

Close to Richmond is the most famous garden in the world, the Royal Botanic Garden of Kew. Whilst it is primarily a

scientific institution for cataloguing plants and training botanists it is also a beautiful place to visit. Possibly its most famous feature designed by Sir William Chambers is the Pagoda situated in the upper part of the gardens. Decimus Burton's Palm House in the centre of the gardens is a particularly fine structure of glass and wrought iron. Kew is a good example of a scientific institution performing a very important function and offering something to the public in terms of a visual and fragrant treat.

Leaving west London to return to Charing Cross, from there you can catch a boat downstream to Greenwich. For centuries this area has been associated with royalty. It was a great favourite with Henry VIII, Mary I and Queen Elizabeth I were born here. Inigo Jones built the Queen's House for Henrietta Maria, wife of Charles I and is now part of the National Maritime Museum. Greenwich hospital, designed by Wren, is a stunning addition to riverside London. Permanently moored by Greenwich pier is Cutty Sark, last of the great tea clippers and Gipsy Moth IV in which Sir Francis Chichester circumnavigated the globe. I would recommend anybody to take a trip down the river but with the bonus of Greenwich at the end the journey is a must.

A book could be written about the grand houses of London's outer areas. Nearly all of them are open to the public, nearly all are situated in parkland and many have permanent exhibitions of paintings, furniture, drawings and so on. Whether you are a student of the period or someone like me who just likes to see how the other half lived and the quality of craftmanship they could afford to surround themselves with, visiting Chiswick or Ham or any of a dozen others like them is a great way of escaping from reality if only for a while. Some of the places mentioned have a Cinderella quality about them, after the ball that is.

opposite A world away from traffic jams yet only four miles away from the city. Hampstead Heath is one of London's great open spaces complete with legends of Dick Turpin.

opposite *The Royal Naval Hospital at Greenwich. The National Health was never like this!*

below *Cutty Sark. As majestic in retirement as she was slicing through the oceans.*

following pages *The combination of the Thames, the landscape and Wren's buildings parting to show Inigo Jones's Queen's House transcends mere architecture.*

Kew Gardens, the Palm House. Decimus Burton's design in glass and wrought iron. Could this be where Sir Joseph Paxton got his idea for the Crystal Palace from?

Richmond Park. Antlered and majestic and not a thought of venison stew in their heads.

bottom *Strand on the Green. Genteel buildings, wispy trees and an impassive river contrast strongly with the Thames in central London.*